DESIGN *and decorate* LIVING ROOMS

Lesley Taylor
with Jill Blake

First published in 1998 by
New Holland (Publishers) Ltd
London • Cape Town • Sydney • Singapore

24 Nutford Place
London W1H 6DQ
United Kingdom

80 McKenzie Street
Cape Town 8001
South Africa

3/2 Aquatic Drive
Frenchs Forest, NSW 2086
Australia

ISBN 1 85368 698 0 (hbk)
ISBN 1 85368 699 9 (pbk)

Managing Editor: Coral Walker
Special photography: Janine Hosegood
Designed by: Grahame Dudley Associates
Editor: Emma Callery

Reproduction by Modern Age Repro House Ltd, Hong Kong
Printed and bound by Tien Wah Press, Singapore

Contents

Introduction

Designing and decorating your living room should give many hours of pleasure, both in the creation and the enjoyment afterwards. This is the room where you are likely to spend a great deal of time sitting and relaxing so it is important that its ambience is conducive to just this. But deciding on what style suits you best and how you should set about recreating it can be very difficult and this is where *Design and Decorate Living Rooms* comes into play.

Armed with this book you can first learn how to work out your needs and make the best use of your space in practical terms. Of course, it is difficult to plan exactly what you need if you are still undecided as to your preferences for the finished decor. The core of this book is given over to helping you, as the Style File on pages 10-63 takes a close look at a great number of different kinds of living room. Ranging from contemporary to country, and traditional to studio living, each section looks in depth at a selection of rooms. The text discusses the main decorative features and, more importantly, how you can achieve the same look in your own home.

The Focus File on pages 64-77 elaborates on the more practical elements of decorating a room. It concentrates on upholstery and soft furnishings, storage, walls and floor coverings, fireplaces and focal points, and lighting. Each aspect of the Focus File is written with the home decorator in mind, giving essential and realistic advice so that you can confidently create a truly stylish living room of your own.

AFRICAN ARK

DIVISIONS

▲ A screen can form a useful division in a large living area; alternatively it can help break up a plain expanse of wall.

been removed. Make full use of these recesses for storage purposes, with free-standing or built-in cupboards at low level – these might house the television set or items for the dining table – and shelves above. The shelves could be flexible (supported on wall-mounted, adjustable brackets) or glass-fronted to display and store precious items. In some dual-purpose rooms, one recess can be used as a work area, with a desk or bureau at lower level, and shelves above.

If you want to create a slightly more definite division between the two areas, consider using a portable folding screen, floor-to-ceiling curtains or vertical Venetian blinds.

Most living rooms need a focal point. Plan similar storage facilities and seating to those described above, even if there is only one chimney breast. You could make a blank wall more interesting with fitted units, leaving space in the centre for a gas or electric fire, or an eye-catching display item. The seating can then be grouped around this.

If there is a beautiful view from the window, you might well prefer to use it as the room's focal point, especially in summer. Group seating around it, but don't block the access to the garden if the window is the main exit route.

As with all rooms, there is really only one way to plan the layout efficiently, and this means making a floor plan to scale, so you can see exactly how the furniture will fit. This looks like a bird's-eye view of the space. Measure up accurately, then draw out the room shape, on squared paper if possible (it is easier this way), making one square on the plan equal to one unit of floor space. For example, if you draw a 1:50 scale plan, this means that 1 cm or 1 inch on the plan equals 50 cm or 50 inches of the actual floor space. Ensure you show recesses, projections, doors and door swings (the way they open), radiators, windows, and anything else that is relevant.

COSY CORNER

▲ A small corner has been used to good advantage by filling it with a cosy seating arrangement. An extending wall lamp provides light to what could otherwise be a rather dark area; it is also ideal for reading.

Then use a separate sheet of squared paper to draw and cut out templates of your existing, or proposed, items of furniture. Remember to use the same scale and move the templates about on the plan until you are happy with the arrangement. You might like to colour-code these, with one set of templates to represent existing items and a different colour for proposed purchases.

If you want to be totally professional and make a clearer plan, trace off the plan/furniture in ink using tracing paper – always write the scale, eg 1:20, 1:50, on the plan. You can then work out your lighting plan (see pages 74-75) on a tracing paper overlay and you can make sure that the task lighting, for example, comes in the right place – say, positioned over the dining table.

Similar scale plans can be made for walls (elevations) to allow you to work out shelving, storage, etc., and to enable you to see whether furniture will fit under windowsills. The wall is drawn as a straight line, with windows, fireplaces and radiators shown flat to scale; furniture templates need to be drawn in profile, as well, and not as though they were seen from above.

STYLE *file*

There is a huge choice of styles from which to choose when decorating any part of your home, but somehow for the living room the choice is especially wide. Do you want to emulate a country or townhouse dwelling? Is your preference for something more contemporary or perhaps for a more traditional, period feel? Do you favour shades that team and tone or bright, primary colours from opposite sides of the colour wheel? Is your taste for simple, streamlined furnishings or for more ornate window treatments with pelmets and tiebacks? Do you like light, airy surroundings or want to nestle down into something a little more cosy and atmospheric? By answering these questions you will start to form ideas for how you would like your living room to look.

LOFT LIVING
▲ Loft spaces are frequently very bright and airy with a large proportion of wall space given over to windows. In this room, maximum play is made of the light by painting the walls and ceiling white. The dark blue in the furnishings and carpet successfully keeps the living area 'grounded'.

Bear all these considerations in mind as you set out on the decorating path and look through each of the sections on the following pages. This part of the book puts different styles into context and it shows you how to recreate the ideas in your own living room. By taking a close look at the basic elements of walls, floors, lighting and soft furnishings, and by mixing style, texture and form, an overall picture emerges. With careful planning, a firm idea of what style you want to recreate, together with attention to detail, you will discover the pleasure of designing and decorating the living room of your dreams.

TOP LEFT
Combine different patterns from the same palette of colours. Here, classic furnishings are brought a touch of modernity through the boldly-striped sofa.

BOTTOM LEFT
A collection of ethnic artefacts and pictures sets the theme. This living room's decor is simply created with suitable furnishing fabric and rugs.

TOP RIGHT
Pale, natural and light painted wood teams with cream-coloured furnishings in this ecletic yet calming mix of styles. Red-brown accents provide a warm touch.

BOTTOM RIGHT
Successful colour scheming here uses warm aqua blue as the dominant colour, offset with a lesser quantity of pale yellow to add contrast.

Contemporary living

PLAINLY UP TO DATE
▲ A plain backdrop is the perfect foil for dramatic pieces of contemporary art and shapely furniture.

Contemporary style means 'of today' and almost anything goes. The style can be frankly modern and minimalist, post-modern or even hi-tech, all of which have their origins in the Arts and Crafts movement at the end of the last century, the work of the architect Le Corbusier in the 1920s and the Bauhaus movement of the 1930s. The aims of all three were to combine the use of natural materials and well-made products with the technology of the machine age.

There are also many other current influences from Europe and from the USA, where the loftspace look, the Californian beach house and Shaker style are proving inspirational. Additionally, Oriental – especially Japanese – style is setting a new pared-down trend, and the ancient Chinese art of location and orientation, feng shui, is being considered more and more.

But the name 'contemporary' has also come to be associated with a simple, uncluttered Scandinavian look. This first became popular in the 1950s after the post-war rash of angular forms, riotous patterns and bold primary colours. Now the look has returned in a more restrained form, using pale colours and woods, natural textures and subtle paint finishes. Above all, the furniture is functional, often fulfilling more than one purpose, leaving the room uncluttered.

Contemporary style can also be highly individual, with the 'shell' of the room decorated simply while making bold use of colour in the furniture and furnishings. Shapes assume a greater importance, especially when used to make a dramatic statement.

ONE-COLOUR LIVING

▶ By using a monochromatic and plain colour scheme teamed with simple ornaments and furnishings, a traditional setting is given a modern look.

TANTILIZING TEXTURES

▼ Wonderful textures and splendid plant specimens combine to create a living room of immense variety and interest.

Animal prints add flair *to a neutral scheme*

STARK CONTRASTS
▲ Black and white patterns are supremely striking when set in a simple, monochromatic colour scheme.

This style can be used to create a room in which it is easy to relax after a hard day's work. The seating is arranged in a comfortable U-shape, to ease conversation, and grouped around a low-level coffee table, which is also used for storage. The coffee table, positioned in front of the seating, is an essential part of the style, and was adapted in the 1950s from a sofa table (which used to be positioned at the back, or drawn up to the side of the sofa for games, say, or to support lamps).

The soft, neutral colours give an impression of space and cool calm. The beiges, creams and off-whites with bleached woods rely on interesting textures and sharply defined contrast of form, to create a stylish sitting room. Even the radiator is coloured to blend unobtrusively into the background. If you choose to paint your radiator to match the background wall, avoid oil-based paints as the colours will discolour and stain in time.

NATURALLY RESTRAINED
▼ Subtle patterns are introduced through the patina of natural timber, textiles and fruits.

Pattern in this contemporary setting is restrained, being confined to an upholstered chair and two geometric abstract pictures, which are not particularly dominant as they are all part of the monochromatic scheme, and thus blend into the background. Instead, tonal contrast is achieved by the darker floor colour, strikingly contrasting patterned cushions and stripped natural wood window frames – a model of understatement.

The window treatment, too, is simple, with neat, narrow-slatted 'micro' blinds that can be angled to diffuse the daylight. Night lighting is provided by pools of light cast from the lamps which sit on the glass storage chests to each side of the sofa, and by wallwashers, which bathe the paintings in a warm glow. Houseplants are used to provide a crisp green accent – very much an integral part of the Scandinavian look.

NEUTRALS

▼ Soft, neutral colours create a sense of calm and peace. Mix beige, buttermilk and oyster colours with bleached woods, using accessories such as plants to provide contrasts.

New chic with crimson, *black and*

CREATIVELY COLOURFUL
▼ The imaginative use of vibrantly coloured glass in many different forms, brings a plain contemporary background vividly to life.

A bold, open-plan living area is typical of a metropolitan contemporary style, and works particularly well in apartments, converted warehouses and loft spaces. The textures are all modern in feel – shiny chrome, marbled flooring, glassware and glazed pottery, natural woven fabrics, leather and suedes – offset by plain, matt emulsion-painted walls and ceiling. Some contemporary interior designers like to make use of glossed surfaces, especially ceilings, to make a greater play of lighting. In this setting, however, there would have been far too much reflection from

coloured glass

CONTRAST
▲ Black, white and red – three of the most strikingly contrasting colours – when combined with reflective and matt surfaces can achieve a visually stimulating interior.

the flooring, and the chrome and glass shelves. You will find that combining matt and shiny surfaces is a valuable asset when varying texture in a living room.

The main decorations are neutral – creamy whites, greys and black – and the smooth flooring is laid in such a way as to help define the different areas in this large living space. This is further enhanced by the change in floor level. Even the main upholstery is monochrome, enlivened by bright red, contrasting cushions.

Vivid splashes of colour add excitement to the scheme and provide a visual link that leads the eye from area to area. Standing by the seating space you are taken from the primary red cushions, to the larger-than-average picture and the collection of glass on the slimline glazed shelves on the wall, to the unusual stained glass panels in the dining area.

The scheme relies on really good lighting for maximum impact. The glass shelves are lit from above by spots and from below with uplighters, and as light shines through the shelves, the collection is enhanced by interesting shadows cast on the wall behind. The picture is similarly highlighted by spotlights set on the ceiling, while the stained glass panels are lit from behind. A floor-standing uplighter is a feature in its own right. This is the archetypal functional piece of furniture that makes a statement in its own right.

Unusual pieces of statuary and a feathery flower arrangement complete the scheme.

Soft furnishings medley *creates rustic charm*

DASHING DISPLAY
▲ If you are without a mantelpiece and want to create something similar, search out a simple shelving unit and display ceramics, glass, or any other objects that you cherish.

The rustic look perfectly complements this country cottage interior, being typical of the timber-framed buildings of hundreds of years ago. This method of building construction is becoming popular again and is well worth considering if you want to create a rustic-style living space.

The ceiling beams are exposed and matt sealed. (Never paint, stain or creosote old beams as this spoils their natural texture and colour.) A mantelshelf is added above the fireplace to tone. The chimney breast and walls are simply plastered and painted off-white – as is the plaster between the ceiling beams – with the brick interior of the fireplace left exposed.

Individual pieces of comfortable upholstered furniture are gathered around this inviting focal point, and are covered in different fabrics. The simple striped woven stool cover, the striped and coordinating floral chintzes on the small armchair and ample, buttoned sofa work well together. Conventional three-piece suites and all-matching items do not work if you want to create a rustic look.

The original tiled floor is covered in oriental rugs – dyed in warm, earthy colours – to provide comfort underfoot. When used on hard floors, such rugs should always have a non-slip backing to prevent 'creeping and curl' and to avoid accidents. If the rugs are coloured using natural dyes, a backing will prevent staining of the floor beneath.

WARM AND INVITING

◀ A very inviting living room has been created through soft and comfortable funishings, a plethora of well-positioned pictures and other accessories, and subtle lighting.

The accessories are chosen to further enhance the rustic theme. The pictures on coloured mounts, all similarly framed, draw attention to the fireplace. The circular occasional tables are covered with textured woven throws, in similar colours to the upholstered stool, and are used to display a cherished collection. When the lamps are lit, they cast pools of light onto these objects, highlighting the pictures mounted on the chimney breast, and bathing the entire seating area in a warm and welcoming glow.

FABRIC HALLMARKS

▼ Soft velvets, brocades and fringed braids in muted colours are hallmarks of the country look.

Personal style

Interior design and decoration can be a highly personal affair. Many people like to create an entirely individual look to stamp their own personality on their surroundings. They prefer to build an eclectic mix by collecting furniture, fabrics, cushions, ornaments, artifacts and other accessories over a period of time.

Adding a personal touch can be an inexpensive way of creating a stunning scheme. It is also a good way of converting rented or company accommodation into a real home, even if there are restrictions on what can be done with the decorations and furniture. Fabrics, throws, rugs, pictures and accessories will all help you achieve the desired result – and they can be taken away with you when you move on.

JUNGLE LIFE
▼ Ethnic accessories sit very comfortably against a yellow background. The palm tree provides an authentic finishing touch.

The result can be one of inspired flair, perhaps brought about by using simple blocks of bold colour against a neutral background. Or think about using various paint finishes and techniques to add that individual touch. A small room with objects and furniture painted like bargeware, for example, will suggest a narrow boat or caravan; stencilled and painted patterns work well in most situations, and add design interest without the need to hang wallpaper. Floors can be similarly treated, or painted to suggest a rug (or use a heavy canvas for this, so that it does not become a permanent fixture).

The patterns and textures provided by fabrics are an easy – and even less permanent – way of creating a highly personalized interior, while pictures will always remain an important way of adding an individual touch.

TRUE DRAMA

▶ Paint effects are a great way of adding a truly personal touch to your living room. They can be as dramatic – as here – or as subtle as you like. If you don't like the end result, all you need to do is paint over the top.

DRAMATIC STATEMENT

▼ This living room is certainly making a dramatic statement. Noel Coward and a pillar-box red piano dominate the background, while the glass-laden coffee table and svelte leopard-skin cushions bring drama to the seating area.

Traditional living

PERFECTLY PERIOD

▼ Regency stripes, a well-dressed wicker sofa and beautiful floral prints transform this living room into a truly traditional setting.

The English classic country house look is currently the height of decorating chic for living rooms, and is envied and copied all over the world. It is a look that works well in a genuine country setting, where it might be scaled down to become 'country cottage' style, but is equally at home in a town house, where it will bring a breath of fresh air.

The country style relies on contrast of texture and form; muted colour schemes; interesting and varied accessories that are well grouped; beautifully draped window treatments, and lots of plants and stunning flower arrangements. The room is then further enhanced with pools of light from table and standard lamps, combined with subtle window lighting.

The end result should look as though the room has been built up over many decades. Furniture can be an eclectic mix, some of it genuine antiques, together with possibly a few reproduction pieces, and other items painted and/or distressed to look as though they are old and part of the whole. Tables may be 'skirted' with fabric and older pieces of upholstery concealed under a throw, and masses of differently shaped cushions piled on sofas and chairs. Covers may well be loose and easy-to-clean: linen-cotton union, in a floral pattern, is a classic favourite.

Walls are often painted and can have a 'split-level' treatment of dado, dado rail, infill, picture rail, frieze and cornice or coving. This works well in large, tall rooms, helping to reduce the apparent height. If the walls are papered, the pattern should be a classic Regency stripe, heraldic design or full-blown floral.

TRUE BLUES

▶ Blue and white is a traditional favourite. Here, collections of blue and white china coordinate with eclectic upholstery.

FORMALITIES

▲ A traditional room graced by a beautiful bowed window is given a classic treatment with antique furniture, full-length window drapes and a rich floor covering.

Studio living

VERSATILITY
▲ A functional day bed and table mean that this studio flat can quickly be transformed into bedroom, dining room or office as the needs arise.

These days, studio living is trendy. Maximum use can be made of one large, well-lit, open space for living, sleeping, eating, dining, relaxing, and entertaining. This has partly been brought about by the shortage of living space and escalating property prices. Nowadays, many warehouses, factories, hospitals and other industrial spaces are converted into studio living spaces. The top floor of the building may lend itself to loft conversion – an area which usually has interesting architectural features like sloping ceilings, unusual windows and fine views.

The interior is often minimal, leaving the owner to add fittings, furniture, storage and style to personal taste. This means careful planning from the outset if you want to create a really workable space. Try to plan from the inside out – work out what you need to accommodate and store, and decide how you can best divide the space so it will function practically.

Aim to divide the space into zones, so that one part of the space is used for dining, another for sitting and relaxing, another for working (if appropriate), and try to organize the sleeping area so it has some privacy.

When it comes to choosing the decor, this type of space lends itself to bold treatments, since there are usually large areas which can take stronger colours and definite patterns. Remember to relate the size of the pattern and strength of the colour to the scale of the surface on which it is to be used.

MAKING THE MOST OF IT

▲ This long, narrow room is cleverly zoned through the use of a blind that can be lowered beside the bed, and a table that can be drawn into the middle of the room.

SMALL SPACE LIVING

◀ A more feminine approach, the bed in this studio flat has been raised and shelves incorporated to make a room within a room.

FOCUS *file*

Once you've had the opportunity to look at general styles of decoration, you will need to focus on the elements that make up the room of your choice. Over the following pages, we look at those parts of the living room that create the whole. The living room is not only the place to relax and sit in comfort, but it is also the one room that is seen most often by guests – after all, this is a space in the home where you can definitely show off your design and decorating skills in force! The upholstery and soft furnishings you choose are vital to the overall look of the room; they must be both easy to maintain, yet attractive and in keeping with the style of decor. As they can be a costly purchase, you might find the helpful advice, overleaf, well worth reading before selecting this most important element of the room. Walls and floors are the largest areas of the room to be decorated, so decisions on paint, wallpaper, and floor covering are, again, of great importance. Recognising the style of decor is the first step, but then, what is the most effective option? The information on pages 68-71 should help you to decide.

Virtually every living room has a focal point. In colder climes, this is nearly always a fireplace; however, in warmer countries, it could be either a large picture window overlooking a beautiful view of an ocean bay, or a painting, mural or display cabinet. Wherever you live, or whatever style of decor you want to replicate, the section on Focal Points, on pages 74-75, makes interesting reading and offers tips on creating a focus to the room.

The living room also needs to house an assortment of per-

sonal and household items. Sideboards, display cabinets, wall units or freestanding cupboards are all discussed in detail on pages 74-75. They can be turned into a feature in their own right or integrated into the decor in an unobtrusive way.

Finally, adequate and attractive lighting is most necessary in the living room, where relaxation and entertainment feature strongly. On pages 76-77, we explain how to plan for effective lighting, and explain why you need different lights in this multi-functional room.

LINES AND SQUARES

▲ Simple shapes and strong, basic colours are an effective but easy way to create a modern look.

SWAGS AND TAILS

▶ The swags and tails on this window covering have been created by cleverly draping a length of fabric around a heavy wooden pole. But do bear in mind the expense of such treatments – the amount of fabric required is considerable.

covers and napery, as well as for cushions and throws. Again, think of the practical aspects and choose fabrics that are easy to clean or launder if they are to be in a much-used situation. Such items often provide an opportunity to bring in some contrasting colour accents to enliven the scheme, or to provide a balance between patterned and plain surfaces. For example, cushions on a modern, square sofa, upholstered in a plain fabric could include large, circular, geometric-patterned cushions, as well as conventional bolsters covered in a smart tartan check, and some square and triangular ones in plain, but interestingly textured, fabric. A Victorian *chaise longue* might be covered in smart, striped mattress ticking and the cushion styles could include patchwork covers, embroidered petit point, silk with tassel trim, and velvet, all in a range of different sizes and shapes. A skirted circular table might have a layered look with a plain chintz cover to the floor in a rich colour; a shorter floral patterned overskirt, and a lace or crochet top layer. Don't underestimate the use of antique textiles for such accessories: these can often be picked up inexpensively in markets, car boot sales and charity and specialist shops, and can be converted to elegant new use to furnish your living room.

For living room windows, options range from simple roller or Venetian blinds, to opulent swags and tails, trimmed with fringe and tied with tassels.The style of the treatment should relate to the architectural style of the room and the overall decorating theme. Conventionally, main living, drawing and dining room curtains reach to the floor, but although this is undoubtably more elegant, it is not always practical. If there is a window seat

COOLING SPACES

◀ A light, transparent fabric that allows sunlight to filter through is perfect for a south-facing room as the curtains can be drawn by day to create a cool atmosphere.

Storage *solutions*

BREAKING UP
▲ A wall of shelves that is given over entirely to books can have a dense, overpowering effect. Aim to break up the area by using parts of it to display much-loved objects.

When it comes to planning living room storage, you need to assess exactly which items you want to put away neatly – and which you might use as part of an attractive display on dressers, shelves, or inside glass-fronted cabinets. Take into consideration the size and weight of all the things you want to store. Large books, for example, cannot be housed in a flimsy, narrow-shelved bookcase.

Your lifestyle, the room's decor and its size and shape will all influence your choice of storage. In a room with projecting chimney breasts, for example, you can make maximum use of the two recesses for base units, or a desk with shelving above; or use them for display cabinets or an imposing bureau bookcase.

The wood or other finish that you select will also help you to enhance the style of the room. Pine shelving and other storage pieces will suit a country-style living room, but mahogany, yew, walnut or satinwood will add elegance to a more formal room. If your theme is modern, then a pale wood such as ash or sycamore, a contemporary paint finish, modern laminates, or industrial materials like rubber, steel, latex or chrome, would all be a stylish choice. And if none of these appeal, or are affordable, you could combine secondhand pieces with built-in cupboards, all painted to blend with the scheme. You might even try a decorative paint finish such as dragging, marbling or stencilling to unify the various items.

Most living rooms need storage space for a wide range of items, from CDs and video tapes to children's toys. In a dual-purpose room, you may need to house even more items, such as computers and stationery – or even spare bedding if the room is a studio or the sofa is to be used for overnight guests.

First of all, decide exactly what you want to put where, then measure everything. You could combine free with tailor made furniture or dress up some junk shop finds. Whichever option you choose, remember to take your tape measure with you when you go shopping, or make a careful note when commissioning a carpenter. You will then ensure that the insides of any storage unit are as practical as possible.

DISGUISE

▲ Hide ugly hardware with elegant drapes hung from a decorative metal frame.

SLEEK SHELVES

▼ Glass shelving and modular wood cabinets provide ultra-modern display storage.

Focal *points*

ANTIQUE AND MODERN
▲ This beautiful fireplace is in itself a focal point. But the addition of a fine Victorian planter filled with foliage, and a striking modern candleholder draw the eye in even more effectively.

SIMPLY DRAWN
▶ Sometimes a simple jug of flowers is enough to draw the eye to a particular feature – here, the old fireplace.

Most living rooms need a focal point around which the seating can be grouped effectively, since furniture is no longer ranged (as it was in the 18th century) around the walls and 'brought up' into the room when required. Traditionally, in cold climates, the focal point was the fireplace or stove, but nowadays it may well be the television set. But there is no reason why an attractive view from a beautiful window, or a picture, mirror or mural should not be an equally effective focal point. As with all good design planning, try to look as objectively as possible at the room to assess its shape, size and character. Aim to enhance its good features and camouflage the bad, and if an existing fireplace or window is worthy of attention, make it the focal point.

A fireplace is still seen as the warm, welcoming heart of the home, even if it is not used for a real fire. There are many alternatives, from gas-powered log-flame effects to wood-burning stoves. Look for a fireplace that is in keeping with the architectural style of the room; or if there are no obvious features, choose one that suggests a particular style. If you have an original fireplace, don't rush to pull it out. It may be possible to restore it, or if it is ugly, you may find a suitable replacement in a salvage yard. There are also many manufacturers offering reproduction fireplaces and surrounds.

In a room without an existing fireplace or chimney breast, a blank wall can often become a focal point. Fill it with storage units and shelves (see page 70-71), leaving a space in the centre for a free-standing fire or stove, or in warmer climates, group plants, large ornaments or photographs in it, perhaps lit with dramatic display lighting. Other wall treatments can be used to create a similar effect, such as a tapestry, kilim or oriental rug, hung from a pole. Or create mock panels using beading or moulding painted in a contrasting or complementary colour to the main wall. You can perhaps fill the centre of the panel with a different wallpaper or another harmonizing paint colour.

If the focal point is the view from the window, then keep the dressing simple: shutters, blinds or a vertical screen. Remember that at night you might want something a little more decorative – alternatively a view over a floodlit garden can be attractive.

SCREEN TO BE SEEN

▲ A stunning glass fire-screen is the focal point of this room in summer. On cold days, the screen can be drawn aside, when the fire itself naturally attracts attention.

Lighting

As most living rooms serve several different purposes, the lighting needs to be as flexible as possible. Aim to have several circuits, separately controlled, and to fix dimmer switches to one or two of them, to help you adjust the lighting for different moods. Have plenty of socket outlets for table and standard lamps to avoid the problem (and danger) of trailing flexes. Other fixed lighting, such as wall lights and pendants, will need to be positioned to light various surfaces clearly. This is why a scale plan of the room (see pages 6-9) is so useful. It helps you plot the position of all the services accurately at the outset. As with most rooms, you will need to install the three main types of

BRIGHT COMBO

▼ In a living room it is essential that you don't limit yourself to one form of lighting alone. Strive to use both functional and atmospheric lights.

lighting: general, ambient and background. If the room has a second door or access to the garden, dual-switch the lights to operate from both points of entry.

Task lighting is necessary to illuminate a dining table without causing glare, to light any desk area, to enable you to see to read or sew, and to see inside wall units and cupboards. Accent or display lighting can be used to light a picture, wall-hanging or a floral display. It is also an attractive way of lighting a collection inside a glass-fronted cabinet, in an alcove or niche, or display shelves. Light shining down or up through glass shelves is always effective. And don't underestimate the use of pelmet lighting above a window to enhance a beautiful fabric or interesting window treatment.

When you are selecting light fittings or lamp shades, always see them lit as well as unlit first. This is because the effect, especially on the colour, can be totally different when the light shines through the fitting or shade. Most fittings will be a permanent fixture, becoming part of the structure of the room. Others, like table lamps and standard lamps are more easily portable, and are usually referred to as decorative lighting. Whatever fittings you choose, they should be in sympathy with the architectural style of the room, and its decorations and furnishings. Eyeball spots in the ceiling, for example, may suit a hi-tech interior, but would look inappropriate in a period home or with country cottage decor.

LOOKING FOR THE UNUSUAL

◀ Now that halogen light is being used more and more, the style of fittings is becoming increasingly wide ranging. Here, frosted-glass sails and a fine metal mesh add a soft and original filter to the white light.

CLASSIC LIGHT

▼ Chandeliers are the epitome of traditional elegance. Antique versions can be expensive, especially when re-wired for today's use. For a less costly option, buy reproduction, straight from the shelves of lighting departments or DIY stores.

Stockists and suppliers

UNITED KINGDOM AND EUROPE

Amdega Conservatories
Faverdale
Darlington
Co Durham DL3 0PW
Tel: 01325 468522

Appeal Blinds
6 Vale Lane
Bedminster
Bristol BS3 5SD
Tel: 0117 963 7734

Artisan
Trade Showroom
4a Union Court
20-22 Union Road
London SW4 6JP
Tel: 0171 498 6974
Fax: 0171 498 2989
(Contemporary and classic curtain rails)

Colefax & Fowler
Tel: 0181 874 6484
(for stockists)

Cope & Timmins Ltd
Head Office
Angel Road Works
Angel Road
Edmonton
London N18 3AY
with branches in Birmingham, Bristol, Glasgow, Leeds and Manchester
(window furnishings)

Crown Paints
Tel: 01254 704951
(for stockists)

Crowson
Headquarters
Crowson House
Bellbrook Park
Uckfield
East Sussex TN22 1QZ
Tel: 01825 761044
(furniture, furnishings and made-to-measure service)

Crucial Trading Ltd
The Market Hall
Craven Arms
Shropshire SY7 9NY
Tel: 01588 673666
(Natural floor coverings)

The Design Archives
Tel: 01202 753248

Designers Guild
267/271 & 277
Kings Road
London SW3 5EN

Domicil
8850 Weingarten
Am Rebhang 2
Germany
Tel: 0751 48832
(Furniture)

Ducal
Andover
Hants SP10 5AZ
Tel: 01264 333666
(Furniture)

Dulux Paints
Tel: 01753 550555
(customer services)

Fired Earth
Twyford Mill
Oxford Road
Adderbury
Oxon OX17 3HP
Tel: 01295 812088
(Tiles, flooring, fabrics)

The General Trading Company
144 Sloane Street
London SW1X 9BL
Tel: 0171 730 0411

Graham & Greene
4,7 & 10 Elgin Crescent
London W11 2JA
Tel: 0171 727 4594
Fax: 0171 729 9717
and
164 Regents Park Road
London NW1 8XN
Tel: 0171 586 2960
Fax: 0171 483 0901

Habitat
Branches throughout UK
Tel: 0171 255 2545

Heal's
196 Tottenham Court Road
London W1P 9LD
Tel: 0171 636 1666

Laura Ashley
Tel: 01686 622116
(customer services)

MacCulloch & Wallis Ltd
25 Dering Street
London W1R 0BH
Tel: 0171 629 0311
(fabrics with extensive range of silks)

Osborne & Little
Tel: 0181 675 2255
(for stockists)

Parador
Postfach 1741
48637 Coesfeld
Germany
Tel: 02541 7360
Fax: 02541 736213
(Storage)

The Pier (Retail) Ltd
Head Office
153 Milton Park
Abingdon
OX14 4SD
Tel: 01235 821088

Pippa Hale/Today Interiors
Hollis Road
Grantham
Lincs NG31 7QH
Tel: 01476 574401
(Furnishing fabrics)

Prêt à Vivre
39-41 Lonsdale Road
Queens Park
London NW6 6RA
Tel: 0171 328 4500
Fax: 0171 328 4515
(curtains, blinds, fabrics)

Poliform SpA
Via Magni 2
I 22044 Inverigo
Italy
Tel: 031 695111
Fax: 031 699444

Pots and Pithoi
The Barns
East Street
Turners Hill
West Sussex RH10 4QQ
Tel: 01342 714793
Fax: 01342 71700
(Plant pots)

Pukka Palace
174 Tower Bridge Road
London SE1
Tel: 0171 234 0000
Fax: 0171 234 0110
(Natural fabrics)

Rolf Benz AG
Halterbacher Strasse 104
72202 Nagold
Germany
Tel: 07452 601-0
(Modern furniture)

Sanderson
Tel: 0181 440 1397
(for enquiries)

Texas Homecare
Homecharm House
Parkfarm
Wellingborough
Northampton
Tel: 01933 679679
(branches throughout the UK)

Viners of Sheffield plc
Viners House
106 Brent Terrace
London NW2 1BZ
Tel: 0181 450 8900

SOUTH AFRICA

Biggie Best
Head Office
1 Fir Street
Observatory
Cape Town
Tel: (0210 448 1264
Fax: (021) 448 7057
(Thirty-nine branches countrywide)

Wardkiss Homecare
Blue Route Centre
Tokai
Cape Town
Tel: (012) 72 5000
and
329 Sydney Road
Durban
Tel: (031) 25 1551
and
38 East Bruger Street
Bloemfontin
Tel: (051) 30 1888
(General hardware)

AUSTRALIA

BBC Hardware
Branches throughout Australia
Contact Head Office
Building A, Cnr
Cambridge & Chester Streets
Epping NSN 2121
Tel: 02 876 0888

HomeHardware
17 branches, contact:
65 Ashmore Road
Alexandria NSW 2015
New South Wales
Tel: 519 9066

Mitre 10
35 branches, contact:
Access Via 12 Dansu Court Hallam
Princess Highway
Victoria 3803
Victoria
Tel: 796 4999

True Value Hardware
15 branches, contact
136 7 Main North Road
Para West Hills SA 5096
South Australia
Tel: 281 2244

True Value Hardware
56 branches, contact
16 Cambridge Street
Rocklea Queensland 4106
Queensland
Tel: 892 0892

Makit Hardware
35 branches, contact
Kimmer Place
Queens Park WA 6107
Tel: 351 8001

NEW ZEALAND

Carpet Court
57 Barrys Point Road
Takapuna
Tel: 09 489 9094

Levene & Co Ltd
Head Office
Harris Road
East Tamaki
Tel: 09 274 4211

Mitre 10
169 Wairu Road
Glenfield
Tel: 09 443 9900

Placemakers
Support Office
150 Marua Road
Panmure
Tel: 09 535 5100

Resene Colour Shops
14 Link Drive
Glenfield
Tel: 09 444 4387

Acknowledgements

The authors and publishers would like to thank the following companies and their PR agencies for their kind assistance in the loan of photographs and props used in this book. We have taken care to ensure that we have acknowledged everyone and we apologise if, in error, we have omitted anyone.

For use of transparencies:
Domicil, page 11tr; Ducal page 11bl; Appeal Blinds page 54; Rolf Benz page 55t; Amdega Conservatories page 55b; Rolf Benz pages 62, 66; Pippa & Hale page 63t; Parador pages 71, 72 and 77t; 73b, Poliform page 73b; Pots and Pithoi page 59.

Picture Credits
Abode: 7, 23t; 64; 74b
Phillip H Ennis Photography: contents/r; 8; 11tl (designer - Dennis Rolland Inc); 13b (designer - Barbara Ostrom Associates); 16 (designer - Audio/Video Interiors); 29t(designer - KAT Interiors/Kathleen Dickelman); 29b (designer - Vince Lattuca); 33 (designer - Barbara Ostrom Associates); 34 (designer - Marge Young Interiors); 36 (designer - Gail Green 11, Inc); 41 (designer - Bennett Weinstock); 69t (designer - Richard Schlesinger Interior Design); 73t (designer - SGH Designs/Stephen & Gail Huberman); 74t ; 75 (designer Vince Lattuca).
Rupert Horrox: 68
Interior Archive: front cover, Interior Archive/Mortimer 9; Interior Archive/Simon Upton 15, 22; Interior Archive/Schulenberg 21, 25t, 26, 38, 42, 45, 47; 67; Interior Archive/Pilkington 37t
International Interiors: Paul Ryan 19; 53; 61; 63b; 65
Mainstream: contents/l, 4/5; 12; 13t; 28
Elizabeth Whiting Associates: 1; 11br; 23b; 30; 37b 49t; 49b; 50, 57, 69b; 70; 76, 77b; Picture Perfect 48;
Zefa: 10, 58

Index

Page numbers in **bold** refer to photographs